THE EPISTLES OF APOLLONIUS OF TYANA

I.—TO EUPHRATES.

As for myself I am on friendly terms with philosophers; with sophists however or low clerks or any such other kind of wretches, I am neither on friendly terms now, and Heaven forbid I should ever be so at any later time. Although this does not apply to you, unless indeed you chance to be one of them, the following words do very much apply to you: heal and remedy your passions, and try to be a philosopher, and not to be jealous of those who really are such, for in your case old age is already at hand and death.

II.—To the same.

FORASMUCH as virtue cometh by nature, by acquirement, by use, each of these may be held to be worthy of acceptation. See then whether you have any one of them, and either give up the teaching of wisdom for the future or at least communicate it freely and for nothing to those who associate with you, for you already have the riches of Megabyzes.

III.—TO THE SAME.

YOU have visited the countries that lie between me and Italy, beginning from Syria, parading yourself in the so-called royal cities. And you had a philosopher's doublet all the time, and a long white beard, but besides that nothing. And now how comes it that you are returning by sea with a full cargo of silver, of gold, of vases of all sorts, of embroidered raiment, of every other sort of ornament, not to mention overweening pride, and boasting and unhappiness? What cargo is this, and what the purport of these strange purchases? Zeno never purchased but dried fruits.

IV.—TO THE SAME.

YOU would need little for your servants, if only they were servants of a philosopher. Nay, you should not even think of purchasing more than you really want, especially as you incur some ill-fame thereby. But since you have once made the mistake, the next best thing would be if you made as much haste as possible to give away some of what you have to others. You will still retain both your fatherland and your friends.

V.—TO THE SAME.

THERE is no need henceforth for any inmate of his garden, or follower of his school to plead the merit of one of the discourses of Epicurus which is entitled: "About Pleasure." For a genuine advocate thereof has turned up in the Porch itself. But if by way of contradiction you should bring out the lectures and tenets of Chrysippus, let me point out to you a certain passage in the Emperor's correspondence, namely this: "Euphrates has taken money of me and has taken it a second time. Now Epicurus would never have taken it."

VI.—TO THE SAME.

I LATELY asked some rich men, if they foster such bitter feelings. And they answered: "How can we do otherwise?" So I asked them what was the reason of their duress, and they blamed their wealth. But you, my poor wretch, only acquired your wealth yesterday.

VII.—TO THE SAME.

AS soon as you have reached Aegae in your hurry, and discharged your ship there, you have to return again post-haste to Italy, where you must fawn as usual upon the sick, the old men, old women, orphans, rich men, dandies, Midas, Getae. For they say that a merchant must let out every reef. For myself, I would rather clear out the salt-cellar in the house of Themis.

VIII.—TO THE SAME.

PERHAPS then you would like to draw up a little indictment of me? I only wish you had the pluck to do so. And you would be able to repeat these hackneyed and obvious accusations: "Apollonius utterly declines to take a bath." Yes, and what's more, he never quits his house and takes care never to soil his feet. "You never see him moving any part of his person." Yes, for he never moves anything except his soul. "He wears his hair long on his head." Well, and so does the Hellene, because he is a Hellene and not a barbarian. "He wears linen raiment." Yes, for this purest garb is that of priests. "He practises divination." Yes, for many are the things we know not, and there is no other way of foreseeing anything that is going to happen. "But such practices are not consonant with philosophy." Nevertheless they befit the deity. "And moreover he eases the flesh of its agonies and allays suffering." You might equally bring this charge against Asclepius. "He eats alone." Yes, and the rest of the world feed. "He uses few words and on few occasions." Yes, for he has a faculty of holding his tongue altogether. "He abstains from all flesh and from eating any animal food." That is surely a proof of his humanity. If you tell me, Euphrates, that you have put these counts into your indictment, you will probably add the following as well: "If there had been any going, he would have taken money as I have, and presents, and civil promotions." If there had been money going, he would not have taken it. " Nay, but he would have taken it for his country." Yes, but that is not one's country which knows not what it hath.

IX.—To Dion.

IF your object is to please, you had better employ flute and lyre than argument; for they are the instruments which are made to minister to pleasure, and the art of doing so is named music. But argument finds out the truth; and at this you should aim in you actions, at this in your words, at least if you are really making a philosophic study of it.

X.—To the same.

SOME people ask the reason why I have left off giving lectures to large audiences. Let all know then, who may be interested to understand such matters: No discourse can be really useful, unless, if it be single, it be also delivered to a single individual. Anyone then who discourses in any other manner is motived by vain glory to discourse.

XI.—To the Chief Councillors of Caesarea.

MEN'S first need is of gods for everything and above everything; their second of cities, for next after the gods we must honour our cities; and if we are men of sense we prefer our cities' welfare. Now if yours were only one city of many, instead of being, as it is, the greatest in Palestine, excelling all others there in size and in laws, and in institutions and in the warlike virtues of ancestors, and still more in the arts and manners of peace, I should still see reason to admire and honour your city more than all others, and so would every man who has any sense.[1] By common report this would be the reason for preferring your city on a comparison of it with the run of cities.[2] But whenever a city leads the way in paying honour to a single individual, and that one who is a stranger, and comes from afar off, seeing that it is a city which honours him, what can the individual do by way of return, and what worthy repayment of yourselves is possible? This perhaps and none other: That if he is a man beloved of the gods by reason of some natural endowment, he should pray that that city may obtain all blessings, and that his prayer may be granted. This I shall never cease to do in your behalf, for I am pleased to see the manners of Hellenism revealing their own excellence, and doing it by means of public inscriptions. But as Apollonides the son of Aphrodisius is a young man of firm and constant character, and worthy to bear your name, I shall endeavour to render him of use to you in every particular, with the help of some good fortune.

---

[1] Or perhaps we should render "by ordinary reasoning."
[2] Perhaps we should read in the Greek π ροκριτιϛκόν, ἂν ᾖ with Olearius and render "for preferring your city, if the object under comparison were an ordinary city."

XII.—TO THE CHIEF COUNCILLORS OF SELEUCIA.

WHATEVER city is so well affected as yours both towards the gods and towards such men as are worthy of acceptation, is both blessed in itself, and contributes to the excellence of those in whose favour it bears witness. Now though it is not difficult to lead the way in displaying graceful good-will, indeed it is the noblest of human acts, it is yet not easy to requite it; nay it is altogether impossible to find a true equivalent, for I imagine that what in time sequence is second, can never in nature be first. Consequently I am obliged to ask heaven to reward you who have shewn yourselves not only my superiors in ability, but also in deeds. For no man could possibly rise to such achievements as yours. It is a further proof of your gracious good-will towards me that you also wish me to visit you, as I would pray to have visited you already. Your envoys are the more precious to me, because they are already my friends, I mean Hieronymus and Zenon.

XIII.—To the same Persons.

STRATON has indeed passed away from among men, and has left upon earth all that he had of mortality; but we who are here, still undergoing punishment, in other words still living, ought to have some concern for his affairs. One of us then must do one thing, another another, and it is our duty to do it now rather than later; for if in the past we were some of us known as his relations, and some of us merely as his friends, now is the time to show with all sincerity that we are really such, nor must we delay doing our duty to an indefinite future, supposing these names meant anything. I myself, however, am desirous in this matter to be especially your friend, and therefore I undertake to bring up myself Alexander who was his son by Seleucis, and to impart to him my own education. And I should certainly have given him money also, who am bestowing what is so much more important, if it were right that he should receive it.

XIV.—To Euphrates.

I HAVE been asked by many people on many occasions, why it is that I have never been sent for to Italy; or if I was sent for, why I did not come thither, like yourself and sundry other people. Now to the first question I shall give no answer, lest some should think that I knew the reason, whereas I am not interested to know it; but as regards the second question why need I say more than that I would rather have been sent for than go? Farewell.

XV.—TO THE SAME.

PLATO has said that true virtue recognises no master. And supposing anyone fails to honour this answer and delight therein, and instead of doing so sells himself for filthy lucre, I say that he but gives himself many masters.

XVI.—TO THE SAME.

YOU think it your duty to call philosophers who follow Pythagoras magicians, and likewise also those who follow Orpheus. For my own part I think that those who follow no matter whom, ought to be called magicians, if only they are determined to be divine and just men.

XVII.—TO THE SAME.

THE Persians give the name of magi to divine beings. A magus then is either a worshipper of the gods or one who is by nature divine. Well, you are no magus, but a man without god.

XVIII.—TO THE SAME.

HERACLITUS the natural philosopher used to say that man is by nature irrational. Well, if this be true, as it is true, then let everyone hide his face who vainly and idly is held in repute.

XIX.—To Scopelianus, the Sophist.

IN all there are five characters in rational discourse: the philosopher, the historian, the advocate, the writer of epistles, the commentator. And when these general characters have been settled, there emerges afresh in sequence of dignity, first he who is peculiar by reason of his own faculties or nature, and there comes second he who is an imitator of the best, supposing he be one of those who lack natural endowment. But the best is both difficult to find and difficult to appraise; consequently his own character is more fitting for each man to assume, so far forth as it is also more lasting.

XX.—TO DOMITIAN.

IF you leave power, and you have it, then it would be well if you also acquired prudence. For supposing you to have prudence, but to lack power, you would have been equally in need of power; for the one of these ever stands in need of the other, just as the eye needs light and light the eye.

XXI.—TO THE SAME.

IT were best you should hold aloof from barbarians, and not aspire to rule them; for it is not right that they being barbarians should find in you a benefactor.

XXII.—To Lesbonax.

YOU should try to be poor as an individual, but to be rich as a member of humanity.

XXIII.—To Crito.

Pythagoras has declared that the divinest thing we have is the healing art. But if the divinest thing is the healing art, then we must take care of the soul as well as of the body; for surely a living creature cannot be in sound health, if in respect of its highest element it be diseased.

XXIV.—To the Presidents of the Olympic Games and to the Elians.

You invite me to attend the games of Olympia, and have sent me envoys to that effect. And I would come to be a spectator of your physical rivalries, if it did not involve my abandoning the greater arena of moral struggle.

XXV.—To the Peloponnesians.

THE second phase of your relations with one another were the Olympic Games, and though in the first phase you were frankly enemies, in this second you still were not friends.

XXVI.—To the Priests in Olympia.

THE gods are in no need of sacrifices. What then can one do in order to win their favour? One can, in my opinion, acquire wisdom, and, so far as one can, do good to such men as deserve it. This pleases the gods; atheists however can offer sacrifice.

XXVII.—To the Priests in Delphi.

THE priests defile the altar with blood, and then some people ask in amazement why our cities are visited with calamities, when they have courted displeasure on the largest scale. O what folly and dulness! Heraclitus was wise, but not even he could persuade the Ephesians not to purge away mud with mud.

XXVIII.—TO THE KING OF THE SCYTHIANS.

ZAMOLXIS was a good man, and inasmuch as he was a disciple of Pythagoras, a philosopher. And if in his time the Roman had been such as he is now, he would have been glad to be friends with him. But if it is for freedom that you think you ought to struggle and make endeavour, make yourself known as a philosopher, that is to say as a free man.

XXIX.—To a Legislator.

FESTIVALS lead to epidemics; for although they refresh men after their toil, they promote gluttony.

XXX.—TO THE ROMAN QUAESTORS.

YOU hold the highest office of the realm. If then you understand how to govern, why are the cities incessantly declining under your régime? But if you do not understand, you ought first to learn, and then to govern.

XXXI.—To the Procurators of Asia.

WHAT is the use of cutting off branches of wild trees whose growth does harm, when you leave the roots alone?

XXXII.—To the Scribes of the Ephesians.

IT is no use decorating your city with statues and elaborate pictures and promenades and theatres, unless there is good sense there as well and law. For although good sense and law may accompany these, they are not the same thing.

XXXIII.—To the Milesians.

YOUR children lack fathers, your youth lack old men, your wives husbands, your husbands rulers, your rulers laws, your laws philosophers, your philosophers gods, your gods faith. Your ancestors were good men; your present estate you may well loathe.

XXXIV.—To the Wise Men in the Museum.

I HAVE been in Argos and Phocis and Locris and in Sicyon and in Megara, and after holding public lectures in the past in those places, I have ceased to do so any more. Why so? If anyone asks me the reason, I must reply to you and to the Muses in the words of the poet: "I have been turned into a barbarian," not "by long sojourning outside Hellas," but by long sojourning in her midst.

XXXV.—To Hestiaeus.

VIRTUE and wealth are with us most opposed to one another; for a diminution of the one leads to an increase of the other, and an increase to a diminution. How then can both at once be united in the same man, except in the imagination of fools, who take wealth even for virtue? Do not then allow men here to misunderstand me so profoundly, nor permit them to consider me rich rather than a philosopher. For I account it most disgraceful that I should be held to travel abroad in search of money, when there are some who, in order to leave a monument of themselves, have not even embraced virtue.

XXXVI.—To Bassus of Corinth.

Praxiteles of Calchis was a madman. On one occasion he came with a drawn sword to my door; and it was yourself who sent him, you a philosopher and president of the Isthmian games. But the reward you were to give him for murdering me was access to your own wife. And, you foul wretch, Bassus, I had on many occasions been your benefactor.

XXXVII.—TO THE SAME.

IF any Corinthian asks, what did the father of Bassus die of, everyone, citizen and sojourner in the land alike, will answer: By poison. And who administered it? Even the neighbours will tell you: The philosopher. And this wretch wept as he followed his father's bier.

XXXVIII.—To the People of Sardis.

YOU award no prizes for good qualities, for what good qualities have you? But if you were inclined to compete for the first prize in vice, you would all win it at once. Who is it that says such things about the people of Sardis? The people of Sardis F themselves. For of the people there, no one is the friend of another, to the extent of denying out of good-will the most monstrous charges.

XXXIX.—To the same People.

THE very names of your social orders are disgusting, witness the Coddari and the Xurisitauri. These are the first names you give your children, and you are lucky to be worthy of them.

XL.—TO THE SAME PEOPLE.

CODDARI, and Xurisitauri. And how are you going to call your daughters and your wives? For they too belong to the same castes, and are more froward than yourselves.

XLI.—TO THE SAME PEOPLE.

YOU cannot expect even your servants to be well-wishers of yourselves, firstly because they are servants, and secondly because most of them belong to castes opposed to your own. For they too, like yourselves, have their pedigrees.

XLII.—To the Platonic Thinkers.

IF anyone offers money to Apollonius, and he considers the donor to be worthy, he will accept it, if he is in need; but for his philosophy he will take no reward, even though he be in want.

XLIII.—To those who are puffed up with Wisdom.

IF anyone professes to be my disciple, let his profession be that he remains within his house, that he abstains from all bathing, that he kills no living creature, nor eats flesh, that he is exempt from feelings of jealousy, of spite, of hatred, of slander, of enmity, in order to bear the name of a free man and belong to their class. For surely he must beware of carrying about a pretence of manners and character and of language which he merely feigns, in order to make others believe that he leads the life which he does not. Farewell.

XLIV.—To Hestiaeus, his Brother.

OTHER men regard me as the equal of the gods, and some of them even as a god, but until now my own country alone ignores me, my country for which in particular I have striven to be distinguished. What wonder is there in this? For not even on you my brothers, as I perceive, has it clearly dawned that I am superior to most men, both in my language and in my character. For otherwise how could you judge me so harshly as to need to be reminded at all of matters about which, as about no others, even the dullest persons are likely to resent instruction, to wit about country and brethren? Nevertheless you must be aware that it is a noble thing to regard the whole earth as your country and all men as your brethren and friends, seeing that they are the family of one God, that they are of one nature, and that there is a communion of each and all in speech, and likewise in feelings, which is the same, no matter how or where a man has been born, whether he is barbarian or whether he is Hellene, so long only as he is a man. But there is, it must be admitted, a kinship which over-rides philosophical theory, and a familiarity which attracts to itself everything that shares it. So the Odysseus of Homer, as they relate, did not prefer even immortality, when a goddess offered it, to Ithaca. And for my own part I notice that this law pervades even the animal kingdom; for there is not a single bird that will sleep away from its own nest, and though the fishermen may drag the tenants of the deep from their lair, yet they will return unless they are overcome. As for wild beasts neither hunger nor satiety induces them to remain outside their holes. And man is one of these creatures that nature hath so produced, even though he bear the name of sage, for whom all the earth may supply everything else, but can never call up before his eyes the sepulchres of his fathers.

XLV.—TO THE SAME.

IF philosophy be the most precious thing in existence, and if we are convinced that we are philosophers, we cannot rightly be supposed to hate our brethren, and that for a mean and illiberal reason. For it appears our misunderstanding is on the point of money; and that is something which we tried to despise, even before we became philosophers; and therefore it is more likely and reasonable that you should suspect me of having neglected to write to you for some other reason than that. For in fact I was as much afraid to write you the truth, because you might think me boastful, as to write you less than the truth, for fear you might think me over-humble; and both of these things are equally annoying no less to brethren than to friends. Now however I have this information to give you. If heaven should perhaps consent, I will, after meeting my friends in Rhodes, shortly depart thence, and return to you towards the end of spring.

XLVI.—To Gordius.

THEY tell me that Hestiaeus has been wronged by yourself in spite of your having been his friend, if indeed you are the friend of anyone. Beware then, my Gordius, lest you find yourself in conflict not with the semblance of a man, but with the reality. My greetings to your son, Aristocleides, who may, I pray, never resemble yourself. And yet you, as a young man, were beyond reproach.

XLVII.—TO THE SENATE AND PEOPLE OF TYANA.

YOU command me to return to you, and I obey. For the greatest compliment a city can pay to one of its own citizens is to recall him in order to do him honour. And during the whole time that I have been away from your city, I have, although it may be presumptuous to say so, striven to win for. you, by my sojourning abroad, good fame and name and good-will and the friendship of distinguished cities, and equally of distinguished men. And if you merit a still wider and higher consideration, it is only myself and my own natural gifts which are capable of an effort involving so much ability and seriousness. Farewell.

XLVIII.—To Diotimus.

YOU make a mistake in supposing that I want anything either from yourself, with whom I have never had anything in common, or from any body else like you, or under like circumstances. But in fact, even what I have expended on any object conducive to your welfare has been inconsiderable. I shall be best pleased, therefore, if you accept my kindness without incurring any expense yourself. For in no other way but this shall I retain my principles intact. And that this is my way, and this my attitude towards all my fellow-citizens, I might almost say towards all men, you can learn from the rest of the citizens who have accepted my kindness, as often as they stood in need thereof, but who have never been asked to make any return. Do not then take it amiss, if I have rebuked my servant as he deserved, for having in the first instance accepted anything, and if he at once handed back to Lysias your friend, and also a friend of my own, what he received, because he did not know personally any of your servants whom you had left behind. But that there are two accounts of me current, and that they will continue to circulate even in the future, need I be surprised? For it is inevitable in the case of everyone at all prominent in any way, that there should be contradictory accounts of him in circulation. It was so with Pythagoras, with Orpheus, with Plato, and with Socrates; not only were contrary statements made about them, but they were embodied in writing as well, and we need not be surprised seeing that even concerning God himself men's accounts differ from one another. However, good men by a sort of natural affinity will accept the truth, just as bad men will accept the opposite, and we can afford to laugh at such people, I mean the worst sort. This much only it is right for the moment to impress upon you about myself, that even the gods have spoken of me as of a divine man, not only on many occasions to private individuals, but also in public. I shall shock you if I speak more or more highly of myself. I pray for your good health.

XLIX.—To Pherucianus.

I AM very delighted with the letters which you have sent me, for they reveal much intimacy and reminiscence of my family; and I am sure that you are most anxious to see me, and to be seen by me. I shall therefore visit you as soon as possible; wherefore please remain at home. And you shall converse with me, when I have arrived at your residence, in preference to any of your other friends and intimates; since it is right that you should do so.

L.—TO EUPHRATES.

EVEN the most wise Pythagoras belonged to the class of demons; but you still seem to me to be utterly remote from philosophy, and from true science, or you would neither abuse that great man, nor persist in hating certain of those who follow him. You should turn to something else now. For "you have missed your cue" in philosophy, "nor have you hit it off" better than Pandarus, when he *Iliad iv. 140* aimed at Menelaus, in the episode of the violation of oaths.

LI.—TO THE SAME PERSON.

THERE are those who rebuke you for having taken money from the Emperor. There would be nothing absurd in their doing so, were it not clear that you have taken money rewards for your philosophy on so many occasions and on such a large scale, and from so many persons, and from people whom you had got to believe that you were a philosopher.

LII.—TO THE SAME PERSON.

IF anyone converses with a Pythagorean, and asks what boons and how many he shall derive from him, I should myself answer as follows: he will acquire legislative science, geometry, astronomy, arithmetic, knowledge of harmony and of music, and of the physician's art, god-like divination in all its branches, and the still better qualities of magnanimity, greatness of soul, magnificence, constancy, reverence, knowledge and not mere opinion of the gods, direct cognisance of demons and not mere faith, friendship with both, independence of spirit, assiduity, frugality, limitation of his needs, quickness of perception, quickness of movement, quickness in breathing, excellence of colour, health, courage, immortality. And from you, Euphrates, what have your companions obtained that they can keep? Surely no more than the excellence which you possess yourself.

LIII.—Claudius, to the Senate of Tyana.

APOLLONIUS your citizen, a Pythagorean philosopher, has made a brilliant sojourn in Hellas, and has done much good to our young men. Having conferred upon him the honours he deserved, and which are proper to good men who are so truly eminent in philosophy, we have desired to manifest to you by letter our good-will. Fare ye well.

LIV.—Apollonius, to the Censors of Rome.

Some of you have taken trouble to provide harbours and public buildings and enclosures and promenades; but neither you yourselves nor your laws evince any solicitude for the children in your cities, or for the young, or for women. Were it not so it would be a fine thing to be one of your subjects.

LV.—APOLLONIUS TO HIS BROTHER.

EVERYTHING when it hath reached maturity hath a natural tendency to vanish away, and this is old age for every man, after which he remaineth no more. Let not therefore the loss of thy wife in the flower of her age grieve thee beyond measure, nor, because such a thing as death is spoken of, imagine that life is superior thereto, when it is altogether inferior in the eyes of one who reflects. Make thyself then the brother of one that is a philosopher, in the common acceptation of the word, and in particular is a Pythagorean and Apollonius, and restore the former estate of thy household. For if we had found anything to blame in thy former wife, we might reasonably expect thee to shrink from another union; but inasmuch as she was consistently holy and pure and attached to her husband and therefore worthy of your regrets, what should lead us to expect that a second wife should not resemble her? Nay she would in all probability be encouraged to improve in virtue by the fact that her predecessor was not forgotten nor wronged by neglect of her memory. And I would pray thee seriously to concern thyself about the condition of thy brethren as up to the present it is. For thy elder brother has never yet had offspring; and though thy younger brother may still look forward to having a child, yet it is only in the far future; and so here are we three sons, the children of a single father, and we three between us have not a single son. Wherefore there is great risk no less for our country than for the life of our posterity. For if we are better than our father,—though of course, so far forth as he was our father, we are worse,—how can we not reasonably expect our descendants to be still better? I trust then that there may be some to whom we may at least hand on our names, as our ancestors devised these for us. For my tears I am not able to write thee more, but I have nothing more important than this to write.

LVI.—TO THE PEOPLE OF SARDIS.

CROESUS lost the empire of the Lydians by crossing the river Halys. He was taken alive, he was bound in chains, he was set upon the high raised pyre, he saw the fire lit and the flames rising aloft. He was saved, for it appeared that he was honoured and valued by the god. What then ensued? This man, your progenitor, and also your king, who had suffered so much that he deserved not to suffer, was invited to the table of his enemy, and became his adviser and well-wisher, his faithful friend. But you, in your relations with your parents, your children, your friends, kinsmen and tribesmen, evince nothing but truceless, implacable, irreconcilable hatred, and worse than this, unholy and godless frenzy. Ye have made yourselves hateful, by neither crossing the Halys, nor receiving among yourselves anyone from outside. And yet earth bears you her fruit. The earth is unjust.

LVII.—To certain learned Publicists.

LIGHT is the presence of fire, without which it could not be. Now fire is itself an affection, and that whereunto it comes, is of course burnt up. But light can only supply its own radiance to our eyes, on condition of using not force to them, but persuasion. Speech therefore in its turn, resembles in its one aspect, fire which is the affection, and in its other, the radiance which is light. And I pray that the latter which is better may be mine, unless indeed that which I speak of is beyond the reach of my prayer.

LVIII.—To Valerius.

THERE is no death of anyone save in appearance only, even as there is no birth of anyone or becoming, except only in appearance. For when a thing passes from essence into nature we consider that there is a birth or becoming, and in the same way that there is death when it passes from nature into essence; though in truth a thing neither comes into being at any time nor is destroyed. But it is only apparent at one time and later on invisible, the former owing to the density of its material, and the latter by the reason of the lightness or tenuity of the essence, which however remains always the same, and is only subject to differences of movement and state. For this is necessarily the characteristic of change caused not by anything outside, but by a conversion of the whole into the parts, and by a return of the parts into the whole, due to the oneness of the universe. But if someone asks: What is this, which is at one time visible, and at another invisible, as it presents itself in the same or in different objects? It may be answered, that it is characteristic of each of the several genera of things here, when it is full, to be apparent to us because of the resistance of its density to our senses, but to be unseen in case it is emptied of its matter by reason of its tenuity, the latter being perforce shed abroad, and flowing away from the eternal measure which confined it; albeit the measure itself is never created nor destroyed.

Why is it then that error has passed unrefuted on such a scale? The reason is that some imagine that they have themselves actively brought about what they have merely suffered and experienced; because they do not understand that a child brought into the world by parents, is not begotten by its parents, any more than what grows by means of the earth grows out of the earth; nor are phenomenal modifications or affections of matter properties of the individual thing, but it is rather the case that each individual thing's affections are properties of a single phenomenon. And this single phenomenon cannot be rightly spoken of or characterised, except we name it the first essence. For this alone is agent and patient, making itself all things unto all and through all, God eternal, which in so far as it takes on the names and person of individuals, forfeits its peculiar character to its prejudice. Now this is of lesser importance; what is of greater is this, that some are apt to weep so soon as ever God arises out of mankind,[3] by mere change of place and not of nature. But in very truth of things, you should not lament another's death, but prize and reverence it. And the highest and only befitting honour you can pay to death, is to resign unto God him that was here, and continue to rule as before over the human beings entrusted to your care. You dishonour yourself if you improve less through your judgment than by lapse of time, seeing that time alleviates the sorrows even of the wicked. High command is the most important of things; and he will best succeed in the most important office, who has first learnt to govern himself. And what piety moreover is there in deprecating that which has happened by the will of God? If there is an order of reality, and there is, and if God presides over it, the just man will not desire to deprecate his blessings; for such conduct savours of avarice and violates that order; but he will consider that what happens is for the best. Go forward then and heal yourself, dispense justice and console the wretched; so will you wipe away men's tears. You must not prefer your private welfare to the public, but the public to your private. And think what manner of consolation is offered you: the entire province has mourned with you for the loss of your son. Reward those who have grieved with you, and you will far sooner reward them by ceasing to mourn than by confining yourself in your

---

[3] The idea is that by death the divine substance which was confined in a personality or name (which was the same thing) is released, so that where there was only a human being, there is now God.

house. "You have no friends?" But you have a son. "What, the one who is just dead (you will ask)?" "Yes," will be the reply of all who reflect; "for that which exists is not lost, but exists by the very fact that it will be for ever. Or would you argue that that which has no existence comes into being? But how can that be without the destruction of that which is?" Another might say, that you are impious and unjust. Impious towards God, and unjust towards your son, nay impious towards him as well as towards God. Would you then learn what death is? Send and slay me the moment I have uttered these words, and unless you can clothe them afresh with flesh, you have there and then made me superior to yourself. You have abundant time, you have a wife who is sensible, devoted to her husband; you are yourself sound in body, take from yourself whatever lacks. One of the ancient Romans, in order to uphold the law and order of his state, slew his own son, and indeed slew him after crowning him. You are a governor of fifty cities, and noblest of the Romans; yet this present humour of yours is such as to prevent you from affording a stable government even to your household, not to speak of cities and provinces. If Apollonius were with you, he would have persuaded Fabulla not to mourn.

LIX.—The King of the Babylonians, Garmos, to Neogyndes, the King of the Indians.

If you were not of a prying disposition, you would not be laying down the law in other people's affairs; nor as sovereign in India would you be playing the judge for Babylonians. For how came you to know anything about my people? But just recently you have made an attempt upon my kingdom, by trying to cajole me with your letters and by insinuating into my realm such magistrates as these, and you try to cloak under the veil of philanthropy your own aggressive designs. But you will not succeed at all, for you cannot deceive me or take me in.

LX.—To Euphrates.

PRAXITELES of Chalcis was a madman. He appeared at my door in Corinth, together with your friend with a sword in his hand. What then is the reason of his attempting my life? For I have never driven off your oxen, seeing that between your philosophy and mine "there intervene very many shadowy mountains and an echoing ."

LXI.—To Lesbonax.

ANACHARSIS the Scythian was a sage, but, if he was a Scythian, then even though he was a Scythian.

LXII.—THE LACEDAEMONIANS TO APOLLONIUS.

WE send you this copy of a decree conferring honour upon yourself, which we have sealed with the public seal, for your recognition thereof.

"The decree of the Lacedaemonians, according to the resolution taken by their senate on the motion of Tyndareus.

"It was resolved by the government and people to make Apollonius the Pythagorean a citizen, and to bestow upon him the right to possess land and houses. And we have also set up an inscribed image, painted and made of bronze, to commemorate his virtues. For this is the way in which our fathers did honour to good men; for they regarded as sons of Lycurgus all who have chosen a way of life in accordance with the will of the gods."

LXIII.—Apollonius To The Ephors And To The Lacedaemonians.

I HAVE seen your men without any beards, with their thighs and legs smooth and white, clad in soft tunics and light, their fingers covered with rings, and their necks bedizened with necklaces, and shod with shoes of Ionic style. I did not therefore recognize your so-called envoys, though your epistle spoke of them as Lacedaemonians.

LXIV.—TO THE SAME.

YOU invite me again and again to reform your laws and your youth. Now the city of Solon does not invite me. Reverence Lycurgus.

LXV.—To Those of the Ephesians who frequented the Temple of Artemis.

YOU are devoted to holy ceremonies no less than to honouring the Emperor. In general I cannot condemn your custom of inviting and being invited to feasts; but I do condemn the people who by night and by day share the home of the goddess, otherwise I should not see issuing thence thieves and robbers and kidnappers and every sort of wretch or sacrilegious rascal; for your temple is just a den of robbers.

LXVI.—To the same Persons.

THERE is come from Hellas a man who was a Hellene by race; and though he was not an Athenian or indeed a native of Megara, yet he had a better name, and was intent upon making his home together with your goddess. So I would have you assign me some place, where I can stay without contracting a need of purificatory rites, though I always remain inside.

LXVII.—To the same Persons.

YOUR temple is thrown open to all who would sacrifice, or offer prayers, or sing hymns, to suppliants, to Hellenes, barbarians, free men, to slaves. Your law is transcendentally divine. I could recognise the tokens of Zeus and of Leto, if these were alone.

LXVIII.—TO THE MILESIANS.

AN earthquake has shaken your land, as has often happened with the countries of many other people. But as the misfortunes which they suffered were unavoidable, so they exhibited towards one another feelings of pity and not of hatred. You alone have hurled against the gods both missiles and fire, and against such gods as people in either case must have, both after danger and before it. Nay more, when a distinguished philosopher of Hellenic race had often warned you publicly of the disaster in store for you, and had foretold the earthquakes that have happened, him, when the god actually shook your land, you began to accuse daily of having brought it about. Alas, for your public folly; and yet your forefather's name was Thales.

LXIX.—TO THE TRALLIANS.

MANY from all parts, some for one reason and some for another, flock to me both young and old. I then scan the nature of each individual and his manners, as closely as I can, and I mark his disposition towards his own city, to see whether it is just or the reverse; but until this day, I do not find that I could prefer to you Trallians either Lydians, or Achaeans or Ionians, or even the people of ancient Hellas, the natives of Thurii, or Crotona, or Tarentum or any others of the peoples of Italy yonder who are called happy, or of any other races. What then is the reason, why, so much approving of yourselves, I yet do not take up my residence among so excellent a people, although I am of your own race? I will tell you on some other occasion; but at present I have only time to praise you, and say how much superior are your leading citizens in virtue and in speech to those of other cities, and still more to those among whom they have been.

LXX.—TO THE PEOPLE OF SAIS.

As Plato says in his Timaeus, you are the descendants of Athenians, though they have expelled from Attica the goddess you have in common with them, who is called Neith by you, but Athene by them. They have ceased to be Hellenes, and why they have ceased to be, I will tell you. No wise and aged man is an Athenian; for no Athenian ever grew a full beard, since you never saw one of them with any at all. The flatterer is at their doors, the sycophant stands before their gates, the pimp even before their long walls, the parasite in front of Munychia and in front of the Piraeus; as for the goddess she has not even Sunium left to her.

LXXI.—TO THE IONIANS.

YOU think that you ought to be called Hellenes because of your pedigrees, and because you were once on a time a colony of them; but just as the Hellenes are characterised by their customs and laws and language and private life so are men in general by their deportment and appearance. But as for you, most of you have abandoned even your names; nay, owing to this recent prosperity of yours, you have forfeited all tokens of your ancestors. It is quite right therefore that the latter should refuse to welcome you even in their tombs, on the ground that you are no longer recognizable by them. For whereas formerly they bore the names of heroes and sea-captains and legislators, they now bear names such as Lucullus and Fabricius and names of other blessed Lucanians. For myself I would rather be called Mimnermus.

LXXII.—To Hestiaeus.

Our father Apollonius had the name of Menodotus thrice over in his pedigree, but you wish to style yourself once for all Lucretius or Lupercus. Of which of these are you the descendant? It is a disgrace to have a person's name without also having his countenance.

LXXIII.—TO THE SAME.

I AM far away by God's will from my country, but I always ponder in my mind my city's affairs. The generation of those who won the first honour hastens to its end, and in future it will be a reign of children, and a little later on of babes. Here then is what we have to fear, lest the state governed by youth should go wrong; but you need not fear, for our lives are over.

LXXIV.—To the Stoics.

BASSUS was beautiful, but starving; although his sire had plenty of money. Accordingly he began by fleeing to Megara with one of his lovers so-called, and who was one of his pimps as well; for both the one lot and the other were in need of food and money for the journey. Then he fled thence and turned up in Syria. There the pretty youth met with a warm welcome from Euphrates, and from anyone else who like Euphrates was in need of the latest beauty, and was ready out of mere regard for that sage to choose for himself so odd an ideal.

LXXV.—To the People of Sardis.

THE son of Alyattes was unable to save his own city and had no resources left, though he was a king, and his name Croesus. Well, I would like to know what sort of lion you have put your trust in, that you should have embraced this truceless war among yourselves, children and youths all alike, full-grown men and aged, nay even maidens and women? One would suppose that yours was a city of the Erinyes rather than of Demeter. For this goddess is a lover of mankind, and I would know what all this spleen of yours is about.

LXXVI.—To the same Persons.

IT is quite right that an old-fashioned philosopher like myself should be anxious to visit a city so old and considerable as your own; and I would willingly have visited it, without waiting for the invitation which so many other cities have sent me, if I had any hopes of reconciling your city with morality, or with nature or with law or with God. And I would have done in any case so much as in me lies; only faction, as some one has remarked, is crueller than war.

LXXVII.—To his Disciples.

Everything that I have ever said, I have said out of consideration for philosophy, and not to please Euphrates. Let no one suppose that I have been afraid of the sword of Praxiteles, or of the poison of Lysias. For this too is the weapon of Euphrates.

LXXVIII.—To Iarchas And His Sages.

... No, by the water of Tantalus in which you initiated me. (Cited by Porphyry, *De Styge*, sub fin.)

LXXIX.—To Euphrates.

THE soul which does not take trouble to train the body to be self-sufficing, is not able to make itself content with little. (From the *Florilegium* of Stobaeus, 10, 64.)

LXXX.—TO THE SAME PERSON.

MEN of light and leading use fewest words; for if babblers felt as much annoyance as they inflict, they would not be so long-winded. (36, 29.)

LXXXI.—To his Disciples.

SIMONIDES used to say that he had never had cause to repent of being silent, though he had often repented of having spoken. (33, 12.)

LXXXII.—TO THE SAME PERSONS.

LOQUACITY has many pit-falls, but silence none.

(36, 28.)

LXXXIII.—To Delius.

To tell a lie is base, to tell the truth is noble.

(II, 20.)

LXXXIV.—To his Disciples.

BELIEVE not that I lightly recommend to others anything. For I myself live upon barley bread, and I suit the rest of my diet to this dish, and I recommend a similar diet to yourselves. (17, 15.)

LXXXV.—To Idomena.

WE have carefully trained ourselves to be content with little, not in order exclusively to use a cheap and common fare, but in order that we may not shrink therefrom. (17, 14.)

LXXXVI.—TO MACEDON.

QUICKNESS of temper blossoms into madness. (20, 49.)

LXXXVII.—To Aristokles.

THE passion of anger, unless it is restrained by social intercourse and so cured, becomes a physical disease. (20, 50.)

LXXXVIII.—TO SATYRUS.

MOST men are as apt to palliate their own offences, as they are to condemn them in other people. (23, 15.)

LXXXIX.—TO DANAUS.

A task once begun never wearies. (29, 83.)

XC.—To Dion.

Not to exist at all is nothing, but to exist is pain and weariness. (18, 82.)

XCI.—To his Brothers.

YOU must not feel envious of anyone; for while good men deserve what they have, the bad live badly even if they are prosperous. (38, 58.)

XCII.—TO DIONYSIUS.

IT is a good thing, before you suffer, to have learnt how great a blessing is tranquillity. (58, 12.)

XCIII.—To Numenius.

WE must not mourn the loss of such good friends, but we must remember that the best part of our life was that which we lived in the society of our friends. (124, 35.)

XCIV.—To Theaetetus.

CONSOLE a mourner by representing to him the ills of other people. (I.24, 37.)

XCV.—To Cornelianus.

LIFE is short for the man who does well, but for him that is unlucky it is long. (121, 34.)

XCVI.—To Democrates.

ONE who shows excessive anger over small offences prevents the offender from distinguishing, when he has offended in lesser things, and when in greater. (20, 51.)

XCVII.—To Lycus.

It is not poverty that is disgraceful by nature, but poverty due to a disgraceful reason is a reproach. (95, 9.)

www.ingramcontent.com/pod-product-compliance
Lightning Source LLC
Chambersburg PA
CBHW071742090426
42738CB00011B/2536